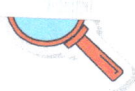

BANK MANAGER

© 2024 Julie Dascoli

All rights reserved. No part of this book may be reproduced or transmitted in any form or by any means, electronic or mechanical, including photocopying, recording or by any information storage and retrieval system, without prior permission in writing from the publisher.

Published in 2024 by Amba Press, Melbourne, Australia.
www.ambapress.com.au

Previously published in 2015 by Hawker Brownlow Education.
This edition replaces all previous editions.

ISBN: 9781923116887 (pbk)
ISBN: 9781923116894 (ebk)

A catalogue record for this book is available from the National Library of Australia.

BANK MANAGER

Written by Julie Dascoli

Photography by Laura Dascoli

Dear Reader,

Welcome to this volume of the *Real People Real Careers* series. I hope you'll enjoy learning about another exciting job people can do.

Before you read on, I'd like to say a few thank-yous to the people who helped to make this book possible.

Firstly, thank you to Laura Dascoli, who took the photographs you see in the book, and to Donna Dascoli, who provided initial editing and computer support services.

Secondly, my thanks to the staff and students in Years 4, 5 and 6 of the Mossgiel Park Primary School class of 2016 for their unwavering help and support.

And finally, I'm doubly grateful to Joseph, who generously gave up his time to help others learn about his profession – and to show them all the ways in which his job rules!

Happy reading!

Julie Dascoli

BANK MANAGER

My name is Joseph. Most people call me Joe. I am a Bank Manager. I went to a local Catholic primary school, and a state secondary school just near my home.

Over years 11 and 12 I did subjects like **Maths**, **Multimedia**, **Systems Technology**, **Graphics** and a **VET course** in **Automotive Studies**. I completed year 12 and did not have any idea what I wanted to do next. I knew I didn't want to go to **university**, but couldn't think of anything that interested me to do as a career.

I enrolled in a **TAFE** course called a **Pre-Apprenticeship** in **Automotive Studies**. I thought maybe I would enjoy being a **Motor Mechanic**. This was a six-month course. I was **simultaneously** doing one day per week **work experience** with a local Motor Mechanic. I learnt a lot during this time. I also continued working a part-time job at a local department store.

Even after completing the TAFE course, I still did not know what I wanted to do. It was by chance that I found an **advertisement** for a **Bank Teller**. This sounded OK, even though it was not something that I had thought of before, so I got together a **resume** and applied for the job.

Not long after, I received a phone call from the bank, and they asked me to come in for an **interview**. During the interview I was told that I had the job.

This was both exciting and nerve-wracking. Initially I did not see this as a long-term career, I thought that I would do it until I found something better.

I did not have to do a course to be a Bank Teller – all of the training I received while I was working on the job. There was a lot to learn, but it was very interesting.

I learned to work with people from all walks of life, and all ages. The customers' needs always varied, and I enjoyed learning how to **converse** with them and help them with all their banking requirements.

As time went on I transferred to a smaller member-owned credit union bank. Here I had the opportunity to do some courses that are provided internally through the bank. These courses were based around **finance**, **management** and **banking**.

I continued to work hard, and it wasn't long before I was offered a **promotion** to a Customer Service Officer. Over time my hard work was constantly rewarded. I accepted several other promotions, including a position as the Assistant Manager.

After working for this organisation for many years, a job became available as the manager of a branch and I applied for it. I was very proud to be offered this position of responsibility. I am now a Bank Manager.

Being a Bank Manager brings with it varied responsibilities. It is my job to ensure the branch runs smoothly day to day. I need to make sure the customers' banking needs are taken care of in accordance with the law and banking policies. I am also responsible for all of the staff that work with me in my branch. My job is to manage any problems they encounter, their applications for holidays and their work performance each day. I am in charge, and all problems must be run by me.

Being a Bank Manager brings with it varied responsibilities.

Tasks I perform every day

- → disarm alarm system to the branch
- → open safe
- → turn on computers
- → check emails
- → staff meetings
- → open doors for the customers
- → oversee goings on in the branch
- → take **appointments** with customers

Interesting facts about my job

- → We see about 100 customers per day.
- → I work 9–10 hours per day.
- → I have half an hour for lunch.
- → The money we take every day gets re-circulated through the bank and the community via shops and **ATMs**.
- → The bank is kept safe with alarms and **CCTV**. All the money is locked away in a **SAFE.**
- → My favourite tasks are helping people achieve their financial goals and training staff.
- → My least favourite task is running out of time to get everything done in a day.

BANK MANAGER

The company provides me with a uniform. It consists of a navy-blue suit and a white shirt, both with the company's logo on the chest pocket. I also wear a tie and black business shoes.

In the summer I can take off my jacket, but it is important that I always maintain a professional appearance while I am around the customers and the other employees.

> It is important that I always maintain a professional appearance while I am around the customers and the other employees.

You could do my job if you:

- → have good leadership qualities
- → are good at decision-making
- → have good communication skills
- → are a team player
- → are good at training and teaching others
- → can communicate well with people of varying ages
- → are good with numbers and basic mathematics

My work desk

BANK MANAGER

Related occupations

- → Bank Teller
- → Assistant Manager
- → Financial Adviser
- → Loans Manager
- → Customer Service Officer

Ergonomic office chair

Joseph continues to be the manager at this member-owned credit union bank. This is his dream job. He is still passionate about cars and uses the skills he learnt when he was younger to take care of his and his family's cars.

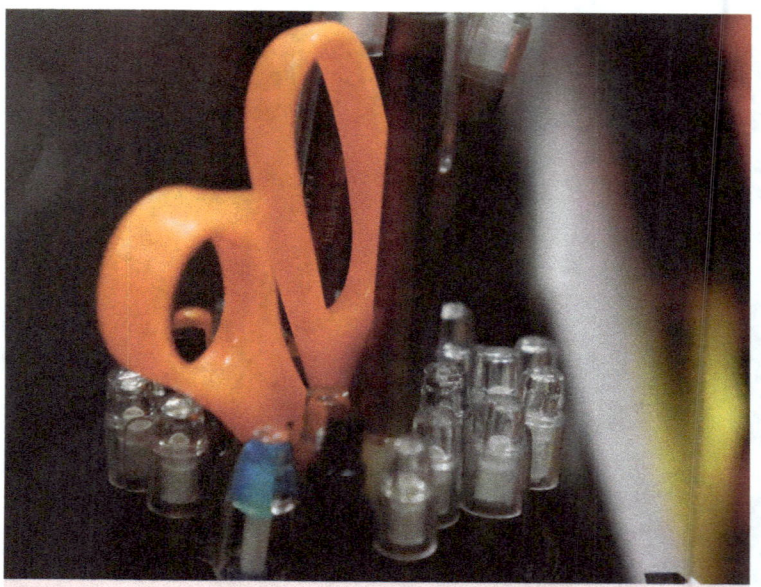

Assorted stationery

Glossary

Advertisement — A notice or announcement to the public promoting a product, service or job vacancy. *Joseph found an advertisement for the bank teller position.*

Appointments — An arrangement to meet with someone face to face at a particular time and place. *A part of Joseph's job is to take appointments with customers so they can discuss their banking needs.*

ATMs — Stands for Automated Teller Machines. An electronic banking outlet which allows customers to make basic transactions without the aid of a bank representative. *The money the bank takes gets re-circulated through ATMs and other sources.*

Automotive Studies — A course designed to prepare the student for a career as a motor mechanic and teach them the basic hand skills required to do the job. *Joseph took Automotive Studies as a VET subject in years 11 and 12.*

Bank Teller — A person who works at a bank and deals directly with most customers. Also known as a cashier. *Joseph found an advertisement for a Bank Teller position.*

Branch	A division or office of a large organisation. *A job became available as a manager of a branch.*
CCTV	Stands for Closed-Circuit Television. A form of security cameras that is constantly monitored. *The banks have CCTV to keep the money safe.*
Converse	Engage in conversation. *Joseph spends a lot of his time conversing with customers.*
Ergonomic chair	A chair designed to take care of the body of the person using it. *Joseph uses an ergonomic chair to take care of his back.*
Finance	The management of large amounts of money. *Joseph did courses on Finance.*
Graphics	The making of drawings in line with the rules of mathematics. *Joseph studied Graphics in high school.*
Interview	A meeting between people face to face. *Joseph had to have an interview with the bank to see if he would be appropriate for the Bank Teller position.*

Management	The process of controlling or dealing with people or things. *Joseph did some courses in management.*
Motor Mechanic	A person who repairs and maintains engines of cars and other vehicles. *Joseph did some work experience and study as a Motor Mechanic.*
Multimedia	The study of combining different forms of text, audio, images or animations for various applications. *Joseph studied Multimedia at high school.*
Pre-Apprenticeship	A course of study undertaken prior to beginning an apprenticeship. The course gives the student a foundation of knowledge about the trade they choose to study. *Joseph enrolled in a Pre-Apprenticeship.*
Promotion	The act of elevating an employee to a position of higher responsibility within the company. *Joseph earned many promotions because he worked very hard.*
Resume	A summary of one's experience, education and skills which is used to give to a potential employer. *Joseph updated his resume so he could apply for the job.*

Safe	A strong fireproof cabinet with a complex lock. *The money is kept in a safe to stop unauthorised people having access to it.*
Simultaneously	To do something at the same time. *Joseph simultaneously studied at TAFE for his pre-apprenticeship and worked one day a week as a Motor Mechanic.*
Staff management	The process of overseeing and coordinating the work of the employees to ensure the bank runs smoothly and effectively. This includes hiring, training and supporting staff, as well as handling any issues that arise to create a positive working environment.
Systems Technology	The study of a vast variety of applications in relation to computers. *Joseph studied Systems Technology at high school.*
TAFE	Technical and Further Education. Courses designed to develop skills in a particular field. *Joseph enrolled in a TAFE course.*
University	A high-level educational institution where students study for degrees. Many occupations require you to hold a degree. *Joseph was sure that he did not want to go to university.*

VET (Vocational Education and Training) course	A TAFE course available for study during high school. The benefit of this is that the student finishes year 12 with a tertiary certificate as well as a high school certificate. *Joseph did a VET course at the same time as year 11 and 12. The course was to lead into being a Motor Mechanic.*
Work experience	Short term experience at a particular workplace, usually for students to get a taste of different careers. *Joseph did work experience as a Motor Mechanic.*

Other titles in this series

  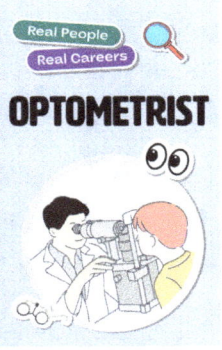

BANK MANAGER   PAGE 19

www.ingramcontent.com/pod-product-compliance
Lightning Source LLC
Chambersburg PA
CBHW070343120526
44590CB00017B/2995